ALL THE COLORS OF ME

PICTURING MY HAPPINESS

KNOWING AND SHOWING MY FEELINGS THROUGH ART

ANNA SHEPHERD
illustrated by ALICIA MÁS

PowerKiDS press.

Published in 2027
by The Rosen Publishing Group, Inc.
2544 Clinton Street, Buffalo, NY 14224

First published in Great Britain in 2023 by Hodder & Stoughton

Credits

Series Editor: Grace Glendinning
Series Designer: Alicia Más
Illustrations: Alicia Más

Cataloging-in-Publication Data

Names: Shepherd, Anna, author. | Más, Alicia, illustrator.
Title: Picturing my happiness / Anna Shepherd, illustrated by Alicia Más.
Description: Buffalo, New York : PowerKids Press, 2027. | Series: All the colors of me
Identifiers: ISBN 9781499458794 (pbk.) | ISBN 9781499458800 (library bound) | ISBN 9781499458817 (ebook)
Subjects: LCSH: Happiness in children--Juvenile literature. | Happiness--Juvenile literature. |
Emotions in children--Juvenile literature.
Classification: LCC BF723.H37 S547 2027 | DDC 155.41242--dc23

Printed in China

CPSIA Compliance Information: Batch #QS27PK. For further information contact Rosen Publishing at 1-800-237-9932.

CONTENTS

LISTENING TO HAPPINESS

Our feelings are so interesting. They are signs telling us about what is going on inside us.

When we feel happy, it means that we like what is happening or what we are thinking about.

LIFE IS GOOD: **we feel SAFE and things are going well.**

Knowing that happiness doesn't stay forever makes us appreciate it even more when it comes around.

You might think that you have no control of your feelings, that they come and they go ... but what if I told you that you can GROW your happiness? It is a skill that you can learn.

Can you think of some times when you have felt really happy? Can you remember why you felt that way? What were you doing?

ART-MAKING CAN HELP

Making art is a great way to feel happy inside.
It is joyful just to play creatively.

Art is also a great way to **show** your feelings because you don't need any words. Sometimes trying to explain things just doesn't hit the spot. A picture might say it better!

There is an expression:

A PICTURE paints a THOUSAND WORDS.

**Have a look at these pictures.
Which feels happier to you?**

Ask yourself, "Why?"

Is it the colors? The shapes? Does each make you think of a story in your head?

Lots of people enjoy making art. It makes them feel happy inside. Why not do some now, just for fun!

You might think, "But I'm no good at art!" (Impossible!) But you don't have to worry about what it will look like. It is all about DOING. Then we see how the DOING helps us understand our feelings.

So let's get creative and see what happens!

We can start by using art to get to know our happiness.

HAPPINESS IS ...

... hard to explain! We don't really need to wonder whether we are feeling happy; we just know it inside. What are some clues that happiness has arrived?

It can feel **warm** in our **chest and tummy**.

We can feel **relaxed** in our body or maybe **tingly** and **full of energy**.

We might feel **friendlier**. Have you ever noticed that?

But where does happiness come from?

Different things will make different people feel happy. Here are some things that might make you feel happy.

BEING WITH LOVED ONES

PLAYING WITH FRIENDS

BEING IN NATURE

EXERCISING

LISTENING TO OR PLAYING MUSIC

MAKING ART

DANCING

What makes YOU really happy? Can you make a picture of some of your ideas?

Think about:

- Shapes you'll use
- Different colors for different examples
- Materials to choose from: pencil, paint, stickers, fabric, or something else
- Textures: smooth or crinkly? Shiny or glittery?

TIP: WHEN TIMES ARE A BIT TRICKY, HAVE A LOOK AT YOUR PICTURES AND REMEMBER THE HAPPY TIMES.

We can also use art and imagination to think more about what

HAPPINESS FEELS LIKE.

Humans experience "happy" in lots of different ways.

Look at this person and imagine it is you.

How do you feel? Perhaps you have butterflies in your tummy? Are you jiggling about on the spot? Do you feel full of excitement?

Now look at this person and imagine it is you.

Do you feel different inside? Have you still got butterflies? Do you feel more settled?

Both pictures are of people who feel happy, but they don't feel the same way, do they?

Ask a trusted adult or friend to help you find a piece of music that makes you feel like the person in the first picture.

What would you call this feeling? Excitement? Glee?

Now try painting while listening to the music. Use colors and patterns that show the feeling.

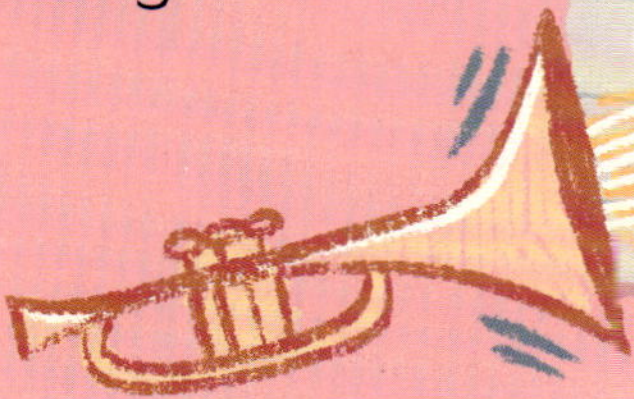

Choose a different piece of music that makes you feel like the person in the second picture.

How would you describe **that** feeling? Peaceful? Content? Again, put the new music on and create a picture that feels like that.

Keep hold of these pictures so you can remember some of the different ways it can feel inside your body when happiness is here.

Art can act like a magic happiness mirror to help us see what our

HAPPINESS LOOKS LIKE

to those around us.

We can often tell if someone is feeling happy – it's an emotion that is hard to hide! You can see it on their face and sense it when you are near them.

We want to be with happy people. It can be catching. Being with happy people can make **us** feel good inside, too.

Try making your happiest face. Take a really good look at yourself in a mirror. Notice what you are doing with your mouth and your eyes.

Now try making your saddest face. Notice your expression and your inside feelings, too.

Can you draw or sculpt a HAPPY you?

Can you draw or sculpt a SAD you?

HAPPY ME

SAD ME

Getting familiar with how your happiness looks and feels compared to your sadness can help you spot both feelings more easily when they come for a visit.

Have you ever thought about what your

HAPPINESS ACTS LIKE?

Which children here are showing their happiness on their faces?

Make a short list or talk to a friend about some of the happiness clues you can spot above.

Not everyone shows their happiness on their face!

Some people might show happiness more with their actions.

How we act when we're happy is different for everyone!

What about YOU? How can we tell when you are happy? Begin drawing a guide to your happiness clues.

Now let's think about different

SHADES OF HAPPINESS.

There are lots of ways we can describe and feel our many happinesses.

HERE ARE SOME WORDS THAT DESCRIBE A WHOLE RANGE OF HAPPY FEELINGS:

ECSTATIC

DELIGHTED

JOYFUL

CHEERFUL

GLAD

LOVING

PEACEFUL

CALM

HAPPY

PLAYFUL

CONTENT

Try making your own Happiness Scale.

Which of the words will go at the very top? How can you show that this is the BIGGEST happy feeling? What color will it be?

Which word will go at the very bottom? What color would you use for that happy feeling?

You could do a drawing next to each of the happiness words to remind you when you feel each one, for example:

GLAD

When my friend wants to play with me.

LOVING

When hugging my dog.

CALM

When I am lying in bed reading.

ECSTATIC

When I score a goal in soccer.

You will come up with your own ideas, too, because **you are wonderfully unique!**

THINKING OF HAPPINESS

is a great way to get more of it in your life.

We all have to **work at** happiness. Being human means seeing things negatively at times. Our brains look out for the bad stuff – they are trying to keep us safe!

Have you ever noticed that you remember the bad things that have happened to you more than the good?

If you are told you are **great** twenty times, you will still remember the **one time** someone said something unkind.

You might also keep thinking about the time when something **embarrassing** happened to you and play it over and over in your head.

We all do these things, but it's not very helpful, is it?

The fantastic news is that you **can** train your brain and change how you think about the world.

You can start by creating your own personal "positivity champion" who can be there when those unhelpful thoughts pop up.

Can you design a character with special happiness skills?

But what happens when we

CAN'T STOP THE HAPPINESS?

What about when we have too much excitement inside?

Have you ever been at a birthday party where it is soooo much fun you can hardly believe it? At first, it feels **fantastic**, but then it can all start to feel a bit too much.

Knowing when your body feels too full of a feeling is a wonderful skill. If you can begin to notice, you might be able to make some changes before it gets overwhelming.

Art-making can be a great way to practice getting those feelings out.

Check that it's OK with an adult, then get some chalk and do BIG marks all over the pavement.

Or use a paintbrush dipped in water to "paint" a fence or a wall with big, stretching strokes.

DOES YOUR BODY FEEL BETTER AFTERWARDS?

Breathing exercises can be a great next step. Draw yourself a "square breathing" poster to hang somewhere you'll see it often.

Try it out when you can throughout your day and see how it feels for you.

Sometimes we might not be able to be happy for a while.
We might need to take care of some other feelings first. Remind yourself that you **will** be happy again.

Have you ever thought about actually

PRACTICING HAPPINESS?

It helps you to remember the good things you have, even when things are going wrong.

Getting into the habit of knowing and showing how we feel can help us all throughout our lives. Here are some great ideas to practice happiness.

Scientists have shown that if you note down **three things** that you **feel grateful** for every night for three weeks, it can increase your happiness.

You could draw your gratitude pictures on sticky notes and post them around your room so you see them every day, even after the three weeks is up!

Another great place to practice happiness is in our imagination – we can do anything there!

Think of all the worlds you can create using just your mind and some art or building materials.

Design and create your dream land, a place where you feel completely happy. Then you can return over and over to your "happy place."

I am sure you can create something AMAZING.

YOU ARE A HAPPINESS ARTIST!

You've done some excellent happiness creativity! It's great to celebrate all your hard work and feel proud of yourself.

You've pictured how you feel happiness inside.

You've pictured what has made you happy in the past.

You've also thought about how to grow your happiness through practice.

Here are even more creative ideas you could try to help your happiness bloom!

Walk or play in nature. Take a sketchbook and draw some of the beautiful scenery to take home.

How about thinking about the WHOLE of your life?

Draw a long line on some paper and write along it all the happy memories you can think of from when you were a little baby until now. Decorate it with happy art and words.

Write and decorate cheerful and kind phrases you can hang on the wall. Make up others if these don't quite fit for you.

I AM KIND

I AM LOVED

I AM UNIQUE

I TAKE CARE OF ALL MY FEELINGS

I AM THOUGHTFUL

I FOCUS ON THE POSITIVE

Why not go to an art gallery or library and find out about different artists' work. If you feel happy when you look at certain pieces, ask yourself, "Why?"

What about making a Happy Hat? Cover it with things that make you smile.

Try putting it on when you are feeling a bit glum. You will smile when you remember the happy things (and it might make you laugh if you look a bit silly)!

Being connected to others is also a big part of feeling happy. Who do you have in your life that you love to be around?

Why not draw a picture of you in the middle of a piece of paper and put all the people that matter most around you?

YOU CAN INCLUDE FAMILY, FRIENDS, PETS, TEACHERS, NEIGHBORS, PEOPLE WHO MIGHT NO LONGER BE ALIVE OR WHO LIVE FAR AWAY ...

BONUS: spread the happiness! You can always give your artwork away as gifts, or design and send a postcard to tell someone why you appreciate them. What a lovely thing for them to receive in the mail!

KEY TERMS

Concentrate: when you focus all your attention on one thing or activity.

Creativity: using your imagination to create something.

Glum: feeling sad or down.

Gratitude: thankfulness for things in your life.

Overwhelming: when a feeling is very strong and it becomes hard to cope.

Pattern: a design or detail that is repeated.

Positivity: being optimistic and hopeful about a situation.

Shades: slightly different varieties of something, such as a color.

Sketch: a simple or quick version of a creative idea.

Sketchbook: a book full of your art ideas.

Texture: the feel or look of the surface of something.

Unique: being the only one of its kind.

BOOKS TO READ

***Kids Can Cope* series,**
by Gill Hasson (Franklin Watts)

- *Bounce Back from Disappointment*
- *Face Your Fears*
- *Let Go of Jealousy*
- *Put Your Worries Away*
- *Say Hi When You're Shy*
- *Step Back from Frustration*
- *Take Charge of Anger*
- *Turn Away from Teasing*

***A World Full of Feelings* series,**
by Louise Spilsbury (Franklin Watts)

- *Finding Calm*
- *Finding Courage*
- *Finding Happiness*
- *Finding Kindness*

***Build Resilience* series,**
by Honor Head (Franklin Watts)

- *Anxiety and Self-esteem*
- *Coping with Change*
- *Friendships and Bullying*
- *Unexpected Challenges*

WEBSITES to **VISIT** with the help of an adult:

Headspace.com

A website and app offering meditation and mindfulness tools to expand on the practice of understanding and dealing with emotions.

Youthmindfulness.org

Resources for mindfulness programs for young people.

HOW TO USE THIS BOOK: A GUIDE FOR ADULTS

This series of art therapy books has been developed to provide a creative starting point for further discussion and exploration around children's emotions.

Each book is intended for children to **share** with trusted adults, whether one-on-one or in a group setting in the classroom or elsewhere.

This book, *Picturing My Happiness*, is an exploration of the look and feel of all kinds of happiness. When dealing with any emotion, big or small, the utmost priority is making children feel **safe and heard** as they think things through.

Whether sharing at home or in a group setting, plan to begin at a time when you and your child or group are relaxed and have an uninterrupted moment to share an activity. It is important that the adult leading the activity is emotionally available when sitting to do this. This can be hard when you feel rushed and stressed, so choose the timing carefully.

Only you will know how much time and energy you and your child or group are able to give to this practice in each session, and what will suit your setting – dip in; read it completely; return to it again at times in the future. No matter what, **don't push things** – try out the bits that your child or group are most drawn to. Have a go at different activities when they feel right for the progression of the individual or group. Use each approach at a time and place that is **most helpful**.

The activities are catalysts for conversations about how children feel. Once the creativity starts flowing, the session may well grow beyond what's in these pages. Maybe a child has their own ideas about ways to feel a bit better that they could share with you or the group? Try to **listen** and not offer unwelcome solutions or critiques. It can be hard when you want to help, but trust that **with love, support and encouragement,** children can usually find their own way through.

Also, take **notice of your own feelings** and responses as your child or group creates, and be mindful that you are modelling how to manage and regulate emotions. You do not need to get it right all the time; **be kind to yourself**, just as we encourage the children to be throughout this book. Helping children is not always easy.

In a group setting it is very important to make sure every child feels safe to share and participate. Establish a rapport of **support** and **zero judgement** of their art and expression of emotion.

But keep in mind that some children may need to have additional, dedicated help beyond what is appropriate to do on your own in a classroom or group setting. See page 32 for quick-reference contacts if you feel your child or group member needs further professional or anonymous assistance.

If you are concerned that a child is struggling to cope, then it is worth seeking advice from a professional.

American Art Therapy Association
arttherapy.org/art-therapist-locator

Learn more about art therapy and find a trained therapist to continue emotional work with a creative approach.

Find a Warmline
www.warmline.org

Warmlines are confidential, free phone services that offer emotional support to people who just need someone to talk to. Find a Warmline near you here.

Kids Help Phone
1-800-668-6868
kidshelpphone.ca

Kids Help Phone is a Canadian e-mental health service for youths with counselors available 24 hours a day.

National Mental Health Hotline
1-866-903-3787
mentalhealthhotline.org

This free, 24-hour help line connects people in need with caring, knowledgeable, licensed mental health counselors.

Nemours Kids Health
kidshealth.org

This website is full of helpful health resources for parents, kids, teens, and educators.